Hearsay

HEARSAY

Lee Robinson

Fordham University Press · New York · 2004

*Library of Congress
Cataloging-in-Publication Data*

Robinson, Lee, 1948–
    Hearsay / Lee Robinson.—1st ed.
        p.   cm.
    ISBN 0-8232-2409-0
    (hardcover)—
    ISBN 0-8232-2410-4 (pbk.)
    I. Title.
    PS3618.O329H43   2004
    811'.6—dc22
    2004011697

Printed in the United States of
America
08 07 06 05 04   5 4 3 2 1
First edition

for Jerry, who husbanded these poems and

for Luke and Sally, the children in them

Acknowledgments

Grateful acknowledgment is made to the editors of the follow-
ing magazines and anthologies, in which these poems were first
published, sometimes in earlier versions:

Appalachia, "Slow Motion," "Black Swallowtail"
Concho River Review, "The Worry Purse"
Explorations (University of Alaska Southeast), "Grief"
Hollins Critic, "The Heaven of Hats"
Is This Forever, or What? Poems and Paintings from Texas,
    ed. by Naomi Nye, Greenwillow Books: "Georgia
    O'Keeffe in Texas"
Iris (University of Virginia), "What I Know"
Point, "Finding The New York Times Book Review at the
    Bowman Truck Stop," "Let Angels Prostrate Fall"
San Antonio Current, "Do You Know That 20% of
    Women Over the Age of 40 Suffer from Problems
    with Bladder Control?"
St. Luke's Review, "Run," "Things Ending with O",
    "Life-Changing Seminars"
South Carolina Poetry Society Yearbook, "Lunch at
    Woolworth's" (winner of the Dubose and Dorothy
    Heyward Society Prize for 2003)
Southern Exposure, "Pictures from a Wedding Book, 1969"
Southern Poetry Review, "Deliverance," "The Morning News"
Tar River Poetry, "After the Hurricane"
Texas Observer, "Work," "Heart's Work," "The Rules of
    Evidence"
Texas Poetry Calendar, "Georgia O'Keeffe in Texas,"
    "Winter Field, South Texas"
Yemassee (University of South Carolina), "The Garden"

Thanks also to the South Carolina Arts Commission, the South
Carolina Poetry Society, the Texas Writers' League and Texas

Arts Commission, Bread Loaf Writers Conference, Gemini Ink (San Antonio), City of Charleston Piccolo Spoleto Festival and the Vermont Studio Center for their support and encouragement; and to Jerry Winakur, Robert Wrigley, Scott Hightower, Wendy Barker, Bonnie Lyons, Sarah Steinhardt, Edmund Robinson, Sally Robinson, Patricia Dwight, Betsy Winakur and Emily Winakur, whose astute and affectionate criticism helped shape this book.

Contents

Foreword

It is probably television that has made the word "hearsay" so widely understood—denotatively, at least, if not within the complexities of jurisprudence—as a legal term. It might have been *Perry Mason* or *Law and Order* or any of the other dozens of crime and court dramas enacted on the little screen over the years, but most of us probably learned about the questionable nature of "hearsay evidence" watching the tube. It is something, we come to see, that lawyers often object to. It is also a delightfully compact English locution, a compound word meaning "something heard from someone else." Among the synonyms offered in most good dictionaries, one will find these: "report," "rumor," "common talk," even "gossip." As evidence, hearsay often seems of limited value.

And yet, in the end, it's all hearsay. Everything. History, biography, the world's holy texts as well as its profane ones; even one's own memory, distilled as it is from actual witness into language, becomes something heard from a someone one no longer happens to be.

In large part, this is, I believe, why poetry is so valuable to a culture. This is why I believe that centuries from now, should the human race survive, it is poetry that will render the hearsay of history into the stories of individual and representative women and men.

Lee Robinson's *Hearsay* is a compendium of the testimonies of a late-twentieth-century American woman. I take the book to be, in part, the autobiography of someone who has done much, seen much, and learned much, but that's not why I love this book. What emerges in the course of these pages is the distillation of human experience into essence, into a measure of sense. It's not that the poems "make sense" of life—that way may indeed lie madness; or heartbreak, at least—it's that they make me *hear* that sense as they say it. I feel, as I read these poems, their rightness, their accuracy. They *say* themselves into my consciousness (and subconscious) in ways that make them not simply the stories of a life that might be Lee Robinson's, but the stories of my own blood and kin and soul, the enactments of what it means to be human. I read and I think, *yes, this is how it is.*

See how skillful is the opening poem, "The Worry Purse." This is no mere prologue; it is extrachronological. The speaker addressing the mother could be of any age and understands that worry for the child is profound and unending. "Go on," Robinson writes in the final couplet of this excellent sonnet, "it's yours. Reach in, you won't be sorry. / Of course I'm fine. (I'm always fine.) Don't worry." That the poem's last word *is* the emotion so designated is perfect, and that it should rhyme with "sorry," thus suggesting the apology it seems to deny, is a preview of just how formally and structurally adroit this poet is.

And, though I hesitate to use the word, how *wise*.

Wisdom in poetry is usually suspect, and for good reason. Most poems that seem to proffer wisdom-in-verse avail themselves of the ready-made idea, the truism, the saw, the cliché. Not so here. As much as anything else, poetry is an act of faith, and Robinson knows this deeply in her bones. In "The Rules of Evidence," she writes:

The history of the world
is hearsay. Hear it.
The whole truth
is unspeakable
and nothing but the truth
is a lie.
I swear this.
My oath is a kiss.
I swear

by everything
incredible.

The poem is nothing less than a formula for living, though it is also an *ars poetica*, a sideways commentary on love, and the sort of advice dispensed by the experienced attorney to the rookie, by the grown woman to anyone who'll hear. That Ms. Robinson knows all about such things is clear, but the wisdom a reader takes from this book is above all the wisdom inherent in the poem, not the poet. Robinson believes the poem must find its own miraculous and unpremeditated end and in so doing transforms itself first, then its maker—its first reader. Thus the conclusion of "Deliverance":

That's [the poem's] deliverance,
its saving grace, and why
when it decides to speak
we listen to a language
that is ours, but so unlike us.

The thing about "hearsay"—and the thing about *Hearsay*, this lovely and finely made collection—is that it presumes and celebrates the two senses most necessary to the poem. The poet hears the poem in the auditory, imaginary spheres, and says it into the air and onto the page; the reader says the poem in his mind's ear or into his own air and hears its resonances, its convictions, its essential persuasion. One is persuaded by these poems because they are full of the world, and alive within the senses. You enter into them and they enter into you, and for the period of that cohabitation, you find yourself changed. It may be "A Dream of Horses" you're hearing, for instance, but soon enough you're in it. It's your dream. See how simply and beautifully it's done:

The moon was full,
the field like snow.

They stood for a long time
looking into the sky,
lifting their heads
as if listening to the stars.

It's a poem about possibility. It's a poem about the blessings
of something beautiful, in the midst of what will not and can-
not last (the dream? beauty? life itself?). It's a poem about tran-
scendence and as such it must itself become transcendent. And
it does. For which we all owe Lee Robinson our gratitude. You
want to know what the stars sound like? Listen up. You'll feel
it in these pages.

As a reader, you can hardly ask for more.

Robert Wrigley
Moscow, Idaho

Hearsay

The Worry Purse

for my mother

I've stayed up all night making this for you,
all night with these felonious scissors slashing
through shivering taffeta, lace, through blue
silk sleeping in your bottom drawer, unsuspecting.
Insomnia's patchwork, it's a fright, won't go
with anything you wear, has a hundred places
a fortune could fall out of. I've stitched it so
the stitches show, so every closure menaces
as much as mends. How clever and compact,
but big enough for children, cars and liquor,
adultery, divorce, a door unlocked,
the unswept chimney's soot, a raging fire.
Go on, it's yours. Reach in, you won't be sorry.
Of course I'm fine. (I'm always fine.) Don't worry.

The Last Fight

Up the stairs, then down, between
the kitchen and the den, I bit,
you punched, we fell a foot or two
then rose to hit or take a hit,

in desperation lunged toward Mama
(humming as she picked a hambone clean)
then down to Daddy, his mood
flickering like the TV screen.

Why didn't they stop us? I screamed
a scream as mean as I could muster
but Huntley Brinkley drowned me out.
I pinched your arm. You pinched me harder.

Blood smeared our shirts, dripped down
our legs. Above, "Swing Low, Sweet Chariot,"
below, portentous talk
about a place called Little Rock.

Minutes stretched into an hour, a week.
In the end we lay down together
sister and brother, neck and neck
in our surrender.

Run

After the speech, alone in the family den—
October, 1962, I was fourteen—
I lay on my back against the cold linoleum
and closed my eyes, imagining
how it might be to kiss the President—
our prince, so elegant and serious, so sure
of himself. I loved the way he said

Even the fruits of victory
will be ashes in our mouth.

Later my father
led us to his basement, until that day
a place off limits to the girls.
Beyond his workshop, deep in the dark,
his flashlight lit the shelter, that little bunker
of our innocence, complete with cans of soup,
water jugs, blankets, Scrabble and Monopoly.
Remember what Kennedy had said?

We must transform the history of man.

Next day my mother took me for the test.
Run, she said, *You'll have half an hour*
to make it home. And run I did, all the way
from the high school to the shopping center,
through neighborhoods of split-levels, spindly
pines, streets like kinfolk who never spoke
to each other: Twisted Laurel, Laurel Lake,
and finally my own Laurel Spring
where with the taste of blood in my mouth
I opened the door three minutes
too late to save myself.

Zack

You remember Zack,
whose mother danced naked
in their living room? She'd turn
the lights down low, play
classical stuff on the stereo.
We'd watch her at night,
through slits in the drapes.
At first we almost choked
on our giggling—she was so
cool and quiet when she drove
carpool. Later
we fell in love with her,
that black hair flying loose,
those long arms spinning.
One by one the rest of you
stopped coming
until it was just me
out there in the dark, kneeling
in the bushes.

You remember Zack.
Nobody else had a mother like that.
He went off to New York
and never came back.

Pictures from a Wedding Book

1969: I marry the banjo boy,
in our parents' church,
with his aunt's ring,
our turquoise
pink lace weeping
mothers, our fathers
grim in black;
uncles, aunts, war hero
cousins, everybody
embarrassing everybody else,
the banjo boy
as pale and mum
as if he is about to be
wheeled in for surgery.
And I—silly in the virgin white—
saying kind things for once
to my sister, who at fourteen
is five-feet-ten
and licking her chops for sex.

Visiting Hour

What we don't say
won't be hushed.
Like the unspeakably red
gladiolas the nurse brings in,
it won't stop blooming:
Daddy, you are dying.

You taught me to shun
unworthy boys,
motorcycles, anything
merely entertaining;
the ordinary ways
of saying things.
Now that I am almost forty
and you are too far gone
to care, I'll tell you
how I longed to get inside
the blue jeans of the boys
from bad families, how
I dreamed you roared at last
out of this dull town
on an enormous Harley,
a cool daddy
in a black leather jacket,

how I screamed *I love you*
at your disappearing back.

Departure

In the woozy room
your wife's face
floats free of her body
as effortlessly
as a balloon rising over rooftops,
its roundness at last
deflating to a dot.

You've always been ready
to leave this world, imagining
the drama of your departure
as if you'd get to watch it
but now you see it's you
who's left behind.

Little by little
things recede. You lose her face,
your tongue, and finally,
your mind. Life,
that ungrateful lover,
will leave before morning,
with no apologies,
not once looking back.

Vernal Equinox

Now in this house
almost nothing moves, my husband's hands
not quite touching the egg that stands upright
on the kitchen counter, suspended
between belief and disbelief,
theory and pure whimsy.

This is the hour of equilibrium, he says,
and I'm too tired to argue. Besides, this day
our daughter conquered space and time
on two wheels only; this night her brother
teeters at the abyss of adolescence
dreaming of breasts just
rising under his girlfriend's blouse.

Tomorrow our eggs
will be scrambled, knees
scraped, breasts fondled,
but tonight the world's on hold.
Come to bed, I say.
It's after midnight.

We'll sleep
in the precarious hammock
hung between desire and regret,
so careful not to rock it.

For My Sister on Her Birthday

I see you riding, then, at eight or nine,
your velvet hat, your brown tweed coat, your hands
held just as you were taught, wrists down, your spine
stiff for the trot, mouth mimicking his commands—
the man who gave the lessons, owned the farm,
who transformed childhood wishes into horses.
Good girl, you listened well, believed in him
who said perfection was the prize for practice.
And now at forty you're astride again.
I want to see you lunge into your years,
lean hard against the withers, leave the ring
and gallop towards the gate, through open pastures,
the pounding hooves not as loud as your heart.
Hold tight, little sister—ride out, ride out!

Slow Motion

Dawn, low tide,
the porpoises
play so close to shore
I worry they may forget
where they are.
A double arc,
they rise in a pair,
one glistening fin
just ahead of the other.
Delight in slow motion,
a slight syncopation,
a flash of sun
on the arched flank,
then another, almost
the same but higher.

Were we once this way?
Or is it memory
that lets us move
so well together then,
who turn now
in our separate lives,
pretending indifference,
both churned in the same
long pounding wave?

Let Angels Prostrate Fall

I think of you, Aunt Etta, dying
at ninety eight in the same room
you've slept in for a decade,

so small and still
the nurse holds her breath
as she leans to listen for yours.

The preacher says you'll turn
from this worldly silence into
an eternal one—his God

reaching down
and trading life for death
as if he'd merely changed the sheets.

Instead, I hear
the great commotion of your soul
rising, the men's choir

at the Methodist Church
in Lancaster, South Carolina, off-key
but strong tonight:

the tenors wild, careening to a fever
pitch, the basses booming loud
and full, and all of them turning

toward the piano bench where you sat
for fifty years, my maiden aunt.
They'll sing you home, Miss Etta,
all heaven clapping.

After the Hurricane
McClellanville, S.C., 1989

REGGIE, 12

They told us all to go to Lincoln High
but we should have knowed not to: that's low ground
there. There was hundreds in the cafeteria
when the water come in. Water come right over
the little children and the grown-ups
was screaming. Everybody got up on the stage
but even there the water was chest-high on me
and still coming, when I don't know who it was
but he got the notion quick to get up into the rafters,
and we hung there, all of us together
until the water come back down. It's a miracle
we didn't drown like that dog who floated in
through the busted window in the pitch-black dark:
the wind done all his howling for him.

RAYMOND, 15

My father got a chair and knocked out the roof
and we climbed up there. When the wind died
we could hear the horns of all them cars
and see their headlights all jumbled up
like some big traffic jam.
When salt water hit them wires
it drove them crazy. Seems like
everything was touched. What was down
is up and what was up is down.
Half the things we had was buried in the mud,
and two caskets floated up out of the ground.
Everything is changed:
old Brother Gathers who's been an invalid for years

got up out of his bed and ran upstairs
when the water first come in.
His house was lifted up and landed
sideways to the road. He says
he kind of likes it, with this new view.
He says he might as well just leave it be.

ANNIE, 68

I don't get around much, with these feet;
I got the sugar and the high blood. See,
they done took two of these toes and I be lucky
it weren't more. I stay here with William—
he's my common law. We been together
long enough to satisfy God. William,
he and me stay. We walk and pray,
we walk and pray.

I lose my two pecan trees
which my first husband
give to me when they was just
little old things. That's what got me
shook up the most, them two trees down
after all the years they'd growed.

God ain't pleased with the way
some people been doing.
Maybe he did this to straighten them out.
It might work on some,
get them closer together,
them that was too far apart.

Our Neighbor Drives Home
after the Hurricane

Halfway there it begins to look bad,
the interstate littered with broken pines,
abandoned cars, a hundred billboards
down, and from the top of the overpass
at the edge of town he can see the roofs
peeled back, tin cans attacked
by some voracious maniac.
He turns onto the boulevard,
past the bloated sloop in its sea of mud,
surveys the shore's new silhouette
for the shape of his house

and there it is—but something huge
and hideous juts up behind it,
an iron arm three stories high, mean
as a Nazi's in its grim salute.
Closer, he can see the barge
that last week inched its way
upriver, the barge with its giant crane
wedged between his house
and the next, blocking the street.

Later he sits on his porch
studying the cold countenance
of the silver water,
water once worthy of his trust, now
like a friend who's turned on him
and goes on living as if nothing's changed.
Reporters ask how it feels to be so lucky:
an inch or two more and the house

would be gone. He doesn't answer.
For days the curious come and go,
all of them perfect strangers
with such familiar faces.

The Garden

Now that the teenagers
have taken the house—
long legs, loud shoes, sarcastic
tongues, their paraphernalia
winding from chair
to floor to stair
like some perverse
unstoppable vine—I retire
to the garden.

Nothing here
talks back. I learn
a language the children
don't speak: *lantana,*
hosta, portulaca. I have gloves
but seldom use them.
I like the dirt
under my fingernails,
the roughness that comes
from pulling weeds,
churning the soil for new beds.

It's time
to pitch the rusty swing set,
to rid the shed of punctured
volleyballs, old bicycles,
a decade of water guns,
time to fill it with peat moss
and new tools:

spade, trowel, rake,
all shiny, all mine.

Woman at the Shore

She lies on her back,
eyes shut. She is her own
vast continent,
mountainous, etched
with deep crevices.

As she turns
to sip her lemonade
something quakes
from deep inside: the tremor
shakes her breasts, travels
through her belly to her thighs.
Her rising from the towel
is against the pull of centuries,

but when she dives
gravity's rusty latch
flies open and the blind
Atlantic lifts her, takes her in
as if she were the smallest thing.

Family Week at Folly Beach

For a week in August the family
comes together by the sea.
This year it's Folly Beach.
The house isn't much,

a sprawling box with a tiny kitchen,
but the bathrooms are clean
and the screened porch, ocean-side,
is wide enough for our expanding crowd.

At sundown on Sunday we gather here—
Can you believe it's been a year?—
to drink our beer and gossip about the one
who's gone to put the dinner on.

By Monday the children know
it's time for an injury—
a sprained knee, a jellyfish sting—
time for something to go wrong,

a crisis to interrupt their mothers' naps,
their fathers' game of poker and perhaps
that silly theorizing
about why the market is or isn't rising.

Mid-week we're all recuperating,
the five-year-old languishing
in a broken chair, sucking his thumb;
his sister, upstairs, wishing she were home.

Friday the second cousins come
"just for a drink" at dinnertime.

We argue about how long to boil
the shrimp, when to serve the meal.

Sunday it's time to pack,
time to move the sofa back
where it was before the children
shoved it to the middle of the room.

We shout *Goodbye, It was wonderful,*
Didn't the children get along well?
Safe in our separate cars we sigh and say
This is the last year. Really.

Now we are gone. The shining ocean
rolls on in its perpetual motion,
heaving, roiling, hissing to a calm,
knowing it will have us back again.

Work

The girl who knelt in that suburban sea of grass, the girl
who combed St. Augustine for weeds, a penny apiece,
what did she learn? That the hues of green are as many
as the million grassy fingers tickling her palm,
that it takes a hundred weeds to make a dollar.

The girl who worked at the branch library, the girl
who shelved books at the library all summer
after seventh grade, what did she learn? That books
are very heavy, even the slim ones. They smell of sex
and death. That there is never enough time to read.

The sophomore who served breakfast in the college
dining hall, who stood like a good soldier before the field
of bacon and eggs, what did she learn? That six
in the morning comes too soon and disappears always
too soon, that the faces of strangers are full of grace.

The senior in the nighttime cleaning crew at the Farmers
and Merchants' National Bank, Boston, 1969, punching
the clock in her blue uniform, what did she learn?
That the restrooms of men are messier than the restrooms
of women, that wastebaskets overflow with secrets.

The graduate teaching English in the middle school,
whose grammar screeched like a frightened animal
pinned against the blackboard, the graduate at 21 before
her class of 35, what lessons did she learn? That nothing
is black and white, that Black and White is everything.

The lawyer just out of law school, tending to the indigent,
the indicted, the three-time housebreaker, the ungrand
   larcener,

to the man who denies he put his cock inside his daughter,
what did she learn? That guilt is what we breathe, as plentiful
as air. That innocence is rare and far more frightening.

The lawyer in her middle age, in her little cage of suit
and stockings, her arms filled with the files of the deserted,
the divorcing, the unsupported and the unsupporting,
what did she learn? That no story is the same as any other,
that love is ever ingenious, always uniquely disappointing.

And the woman who sits at the kitchen window, the woman
who is finished with offices, who sits at the table, whose
window is the world and whose work is this poem, what
does she know? That this is her fortune—this poem, made
word by word, beginning with the girl who kneels in the grass,
beginning with the girl on her knees in the grass.

The Rules of Evidence

What you want to say most
is inadmissible.
Say it anyway.
Say it again.
What they tell you is irrelevant
can't be denied and will
eventually be heard.
Every question
is a leading question.
Ask it anyway, then expect
what you won't get.
There is no such thing
as the original
so you'll have to make do
with a reasonable facsimile.
The history of the world
is hearsay. Hear it.
The whole truth
is unspeakable
and nothing but the truth
is a lie.
I swear this.
My oath is a kiss.
I swear
by everything
incredible.

The Client

She is not
a syndrome
with her wild eyes

one of which explodes
and spills its secrets
on her cheek:

blue
for the days she waited
knowing what would happen

green
for the chance
it wouldn't

yellow for the lucky mornings
nothing but sunlight
touched her while she slept

It isn't black, this eye,
not black, which would be
easier, which might
be night, might be the shade
pulled down to block the memory

not black, which is what
this eye would wear
if it could close for good,
if it could die

Die, as she says,
and be done with it.

The Institutions of Marriage

i.

In the dusty classroom
at the University of Sex
the fat books open like labia
excited at her touch. Around her
the legs of her classmates,
bare and restless through the lecture,
reach out to take her in.
It's only April, but already
hot. Her head pounds from hushing
the voice of her wish:
Choose me, choose me.

ii.

At the asylum where she's taken
by kind men in white, everything
is white: the walls, the sheets,
the many pages of the journal
she won't write in. White,
the matron says, has no opinions,
does not offend. She catches herself
in the tall mirror of the reception area
(it's the last time she remembers
having a face) and there she is
in her mother's wedding gown, so white
the sight of it sends her screaming.

iii.

She's walked a long way to get here,
this Museum of Long Marriages,
through rocky, disconsolate country,

and now there are so many steps—
slick and steep.
Is her old heart up to it?
She could always give up, turn back,
say *to hell with it*
but something keeps her going.
Is it the memory of all those lovely things?
Inside
she finds the marble Greek, a god
who all this time was just a boy,
and the room of Renoir's women,
no longer serene as she remembers them.
Her life spins around her
like Van Gogh's starry sky.

It's time to go. In the atrium
the sound of Bach on the harpsichord,
the odor of gardenias
through the revolving door.

Grounds for Divorce

These are our grounds,
says the lawyer, as if
they could share this grief.
The client's eyes find the window
behind his bobbing head.

First, adultery:
Out there, a garden of delights,
everything green, about
to flower. Primitive, Rousseau.
Eve sings to the snake and neither
cares about Adam,
who is this fellow in the three-piece suit,
this lawyer lecturing.

Physical cruelty, he says,
is difficult to prove.
A sudden tempest blows the window shut.
Rain beats the glass.
*We'll need to show repeated abuse, or short
of that, a life-threatening attack.*
Outside, in what was once
the garden, wind rips the grass from its roots,
sucks whole trees into the sky. Afterwards,
the bruised earth sleeps and for mile after mile
there is nothing but loss, like the eerie streets
of de Chirico.

Habitual drunkenness, he continues,
hissing the last syllable,
includes drug abuse. His eyebrows

rise into question marks. *Are you hot?*
I'll open the window.
Below, on the bench in the littered
park, a wino drains the last of his wine,
throws the bottle into the street.
At the sound of glass splintering
she is her schoolgirl self again,
the smallest one
in the group at the museum, faint
at the sight of the absinthe drinker's face.

Now, he says, *I've saved the easiest*
for last. It's what we call 'no fault'—
a year without cohabitation.
He checks his notes, the form
she filled out in the waiting room.
Looks like we're almost there!
Through the window she can see
the sign blinking from the restaurant:
Open. Inside, she is the only customer,
a figure more alone
than even Hopper could imagine.
There she will wait for the year to be over.
The waiter looks oddly like her lawyer.
He fills her coffee cup and takes her money.
She knows without asking
he doesn't want to hear her story.

Heart's Work

We forget how hard it is, heart's work,
how she sweats in the thankless breast
pushing her mop and pail—
spilling and sucking, sucking
and spilling—without reward,
with nothing but raw will to keep doing
what she's always been doing.

We forget there is no Saturday
for her, even as we lounge
in the grass beside the river
and later sleep in our warm,
clean sheets; forget
how she stays up
stoking the fire, bends over it
with bellows—in and out,
take and give.

Love, she whispers,
so as not to wake us.
Live.

Lunch at Woolworth's

Charleston, S.C., 1996

In such a public place it is a miracle to be alone.
I don't know anybody here, and that is why I come.
Nobody knows me, nobody cares if I have money
or not. I'm just one more for lunch, just "Honey."
The woman behind the counter is a caricature
with her drawn-on brows and her helmet of hair,
those beefy arms laying out my fork and knife.
I don't want the complication of her name, her life,
and so I won't look her in the eye. Of course the tea
comes already sweetened and the meat is leathery.
Today the "choice of vegetables" is not a choice at all:
beans and mashed potatoes. "Potatoes aren't vegetables,"
I almost say, but I don't want to pick a fight.
With the bent fork I poke a hole in the mound of white
and watch the gravy penetrate. Then I notice her,
the little girl hugging her mother's knees, under the counter.
My first thought is of hunger, some abuse
or neglect that would explain this face,
these huge eyes, her solid stare, her fix on me.
But there's no misery here, only curiosity.
What does she think? That I am white, a woman
neither old nor young but somewhere in between?
Does she hate my kind, or does she wish
she could be born again in different flesh?
No. The shame's all mine, the attitude as ingrown
as the rebel flag that won't come down.
Thirty years ago her people sat where I sit,
wanting more than just something to eat;

now I am the object of their grandchild's stare.
That she can make of me what she wishes is the wonder
of her age—that she can look at me and make me happen
like a made-up story, unfold me like the fallen napkin.

Finding *The New York Times Book Review* at the Bowman Truck Stop

The business here is fuel: diesel,
sweet tea, meat and three vegetables,
choice of cornbread or dinner roll.
Not much time for talk, and if there is
it's how are the kids and the bad wreck
up the road. Then what is Stephen Spender
doing here, John Irving imagining
Bombay circuses; Gail Godwin, Yitzhak
Shamir, perverse desire and the politics of art,
all here at my table, Exit 165 off I-26,
halfway from Charleston to Columbia
and about as near to nowhere
as you can get?

Once my half hour here was a respite
from the fast lane, a greasy way-station
in my low-fat life. With my plate of chicken,
rice and beans and turnip greens
I could be as sloppy and happy
as the pot-bellied truckers
licking real butter off their fingers.

So tell me
who left *Same Sex Unions in Premodern Europe*
exposed at my table, *Midnight
in the Garden of Good and Evil*
spotted with grease,
down this week from Number 2
to Number 4?

What the Muse Is Doing When She Can't Come to You

There's the laundry—
a Mount Olympus
of laundry, all those
diaphanous robes
to be done by hand,
then a trip to the market
because she's out of honey,

lunch with her sisters
which goes on far too long
(consoling poor Calliope, whose
wayward offspring Orpheus
has run off to the Styx again,
and serious talk about whether
Father Zeus and Mother Memory
need to go to the nursing home
now that he's missing his mark
with his lightning bolts and she's
beginning to lose her marbles)

then the lessons, the obligatory
hour with the flute
and later a frustrating session
with the voice instructor.
It's demanding and exhausting,
this life of the Muse, so don't
berate her when she comes to you

murmuring excuses, doing
her best to inspire you
though her heart's
not in it.

Family Portrait

No one recalls the occasion now,
two of them gone, another's memory
not what it used to be, and the baby
too young then to remember anything,
but it was January, 1950, says the note
on the back of the photograph,
four generations sit on the old one's sofa
in Orangeburg, South Carolina,
the great-grandmother
with her white hair pinned
in an unseen bun and her lace-up shoes
as prim as her dress;
the grandmother in her Sunday best,
not a thread of it frivolous, and the mother,
twenty-four, in her black wool suit
and sensible pumps,
with the baby on her lap.

Four pairs of eyes
look past the camera,
out there
where the old one drops
among her backyard hens, face
in the dirt, hands balled
into fists, *out there*
where the cancer spark catches
inside the grandmother—
a southern lady, she'll keep it secret
while it burns a hole through her breast—
and still those eyes stare down the years
where the mother, seeing Jackie

with Jack's ruined head in her lap
vows to be always as brave as that,
never, ever to cry
because crying, she says,
is a waste of time and time is busy
turning the baby, me,
into a woman who at fifty-five
looks up from sweeping
and sees the picture
in its silver frame.

Deliverance

There's no such thing
as the necessary poem;
that's what saves poetry
from a life like ours,
from desire and striving.
That is not to say a poem
can't yearn for something
it isn't yet, can't crave
a meal of only apricots
or want a one-way ticket
to another country.
It can. We know
how a poem can need so much
it turns to mush, and how
sometimes even out of mud
and mildew rise the most
fantastic flowers. No,
what I mean is different.
That the poem is redeemed
by indifference, that before
it's written, the world
does very well without it.
Therefore it is free
to be what it wants to be
or not to be at all.
That's its deliverance,
its saving grace, and why
when it decides to speak
we listen to a language
that is ours, but so unlike us.

It Is Worse

for the poet
than for others
to be dead.

No matter how many
still turn her pages,
how well-read

her books,
there is no iamb
in the empty lung.

Though others, too, expire,
the lyric throat abhors
the choking more.

What's said is all there is.
No chance to renounce
the loud-mouthed critics,

and no revision.

Rehearsal at Bread Loaf

Behind you in the blue parlor
voices without faces
rehearse a madrigal.
They sing and stop—
sopranos off—and sing again.
Sometimes the tenors fly
like angels, sometimes
fall flat. This goes on for days.

How long
have you been looking for your life
as if it belonged to someone else?

Suppose this is all there is:
Vermont,
the porch of an inn,
green wooden chair, your feet
and beyond your feet
the road,
the hayfield folding itself
into the river, the hill
and her family of trees,
and over and over,
the madrigal?

w from nature, Art Nouveau and her interior life

...nter Frantise... Russian Kazimir Malevic... eir different ways achieving velocity on canvas. And so was ...dinsky, who would become the most ...eless apostle of an art that answered to ...othing in the merely material world. Born in 1866 to a prosperous Moscow family, Kandinsky spent his 20s studying law and economics, all the while bending toward another calling. He was the sort of young man who could be sent into ecstasies by a sunset. "The sun dissolves the whole of Moscow into a single spot," was how he de- scribed one years later, "which," like a wild tuba, sets all one's soul vibrating." A wild tuba? So much for law and economics.

In 1896, Kandinsky, with his first wife Anja, decamped to Munich to become an artist and art teacher. His early paint-

er of the
tives of
were als
abstract
ing full s
Picture w
And by t
Rider. (B
like-mi
Marc,
he for
blems
Moun
F
alon
wa
e

Grief

"It might be possible to take up a pencil."
—DONALD HALL, *Without*

Can he furnish this dark cottage with words?
Can he make it, if not her home again, at least
a place of temporary comforts, familiar things
she might stop to touch if she came back—
vowels, soft as pillows, still hollow
from the press of her cheek; consonants
like oak, sturdy as the chair that would hold
her aching back. Can he make the bed
she'd lie in, turning the sheet expectantly
like a page in a book he has yet to write?
In his sleep he cries out for her as if she were
the one word he has always been looking for.

The Red Hat

It made me happy just
to look at it—so pert
and proud in the shop,
so unabashedly
scarlet—so I bought
the red hat.

Mondays I wear it
to work, to ease my head
into the office. Midweek
I sometimes put it on at home.
Of course it's silly to sit
in the kitchen with a hat on
but its weight is like a big warm hand
and keeps what's underneath
from spinning.

And it's a good hat
to say goodbye in, leaving you
on Sunday. You can follow it
up the escalator to my flight,
I can watch you
watch it disappear.

The red hat knows nothing of loss,
doesn't love what it can't have.
The red hat is never tired, never
sad. The red hat doesn't blink.
The red hat is always brave.

The Blue Hat

The blue hat knows he must
forget the Brooklyn factory,
the seamstress bent over him
with her bitten nails and dull eyes.
It was an inauspicious birthplace
and he is amazed to find himself
riding along the Champs-Elysée
atop this head which lifts him
almost to heaven.

The woman, too, has come
a long way, wants more
than she can ever have.
From where he sits he can hear
her desire: often she thinks
of her lover—not any of these men
who pass her now,
but an imaginary man, wise
and wild enough to love the tilt
of her head, her long stride,
her hat.

The Heaven of Hats

Now that the self has been shed, he knows
who he really is, this sweet oblivion
as familiar as the black suit they buried him in.
At ease at last with his forgetfulness,
he remembers and is remembered.
The hats come, each one floating up
to greet him, these old friends
left in airport lounges, in moldy closets
of cheap apartments, in hotel rooms
he borrowed for lust and left for love.
Each one finds his bald head and hugs it:
the red knit, the Irish cap, the battered
panama. He thinks *Why hats?* And then,
remembering he's dead, he lets the question
go where all unanswered questions go.
Alone again, he is oddly comforted.
All the lost hats have been found.
All the lost hats have come home.

Invisible Mother

Do you feel my fingers
lift your eyelids at dawn, hear
my voice in your head as you shower,
saying *Don't forget to turn the oven off?*

I ride in your pocket to the office where
all day long I sit on your shoulder.
The boss feels my vigilance, keeps
his hands to himself.

Odorless, colorless, lighter than air,
millions of me could fit on the head
of a pin. My tiny heart is inexhaustible.
My eyes see everything.

Home with you again, I put your shoes away
and straighten the blouse on its hanger.
It is from me you get the recipe
you think you've improvised.

When he comes—the one you say
you love—I let him in, easing his key
in the lock. Just because
I sleep between your sheets,

in the spaces between touching,
don't think I mean to pry. I feel
for you but am not felt. He'll never know,
nor you, who shows him what to do.

Life-Changing Seminars

Happiness, Love and Luck is what she leaves behind,
and *A Positive Balance of Body and Mind.*
She was close enough for me to feel
the soft flesh of her abundant thigh, to smell

the sweat and smoke on the blouse that lacked
a button where her breasts, two large cats,
perched on the sill of her too-small bra. What promise
did she take with her, tearing it from page 26

of "Life-Changing Seminars" just before she got off
at Grand Central? Not *Learn to Love Yourself*
in one lesson only, November 9th, from six to eight,
and not *Hypnotic Trance: Your Key to Losing Weight.*

Communicating with the Dead did not intrigue her,
nor *Twelve Steps to Irresistible Charisma.*
She left the booklet on the seat beside me, a hole
in the newsprint where—with something like a smile

but also the practiced grimace of one who knows
how to hold her pain—she took the fix for her sorrows.
I am on my way downtown, F train, to see my daughter.
I want to tell her what I know about love, what my mother

didn't tell me, that we learn the same lesson over and over,
our hearts breakable as chalk and time no sure eraser.
I want to save her the heartache of believing love alone
can save her, but keep her from the sure doom

of thinking she can do without it. She will listen and smile.
I can see her face already, something in it of the girl
who sat beside me, a stranger, a life of her own,
who took her secrets with her when she left the train.

Stolen Tomatoes

We'd done none of the hard work,
hadn't come daily to stake
the tender plants, to water and weed.
We were just out for a walk,

wanting nothing except
to be together, and there they were,
so big—almost bursting
their skins—and so red.

Later
we sliced the fruits of our theft
and watched the bread
turn bloody.

They were good,
weren't they? And we were happy
to be so full, to be
so bad.

Things Ending with O

It's Friday, the traffic
thick with the five o'clock flock
until San Antonio suburbs fade into fields
and the interstate arches like a rod
casting his truck into the hills. This
is his exit, the house where his life
waits like a faithful dog, a good place
to be a good man, or try to be.
Isn't it more than most men have?
But the sign for El Paso
keeps him on the road, straight
into the sun and its mirages.

It's a long time now between
rest stops, no gasoline for miles.
He could die here, alone.
He drives on, the radio
searching for stations, finding only
fuzzy born-agains, bluegrass,
noise. He turns it off, listens
to the wind against the windows.
Could he live here, alone?

He should call. Dinner
must be almost on, her fingernails
tapping the tabletop as she sips her wine,
but something about the sound of El Paso
keeps him going: El Paso, San Diego,
the sound of his own
amazement after sex:
O yes, and O so long ago

San Diego,
the ocean's blue adagio
taking him in,
letting him go.

Moving

She can't wait for it to be over:
the boxes, the bending,
the goddam tape splitting
as she pulls it from the roll,
the decisions—what to keep?
what to throw away?—
the garbage
too heavy for her to haul alone
though she does it anyway
as a sort of penance
before the movers come.

This is what she dreaded,
but when she's done,
her debris on the street
a mountain of broken promises,
it's the emptiness of the house
that catches her off guard,
each room a testament
to her vanishing, each echoing
how fast a woman can disappear.

To His Daughters

You know my name and not much more
than the one unforgettable fact:
for love of me he's left your mother.
The intricate tangle of cause and effect,

fault's web I'm woven into, didn't spin—
all this eludes you now. I'm the spider
trespassing in your pristine home, coming
through the crack you never knew was there.

Curse me, curse him. Say you hate him,
cry yourself to sleep and wake to crying.
Hate me. I know you must. Imagine,
as I would if I were you, me dying,

your father coming back chagrined,
your mother taking him, forgiving,
the house restored and humming again
with the comfortable noises of living.

I have no right to speak and what I say
will be all wrong. I'll say it anyway:

You'll live, and looking back, bless him
for breaking your hearts, for wreaking
his havoc until they burst wide open,
letting so much out, letting so much in.

What I Know

What I know for sure is less and less:
that a hot bath won't cure loneliness.

That bacon is the best bad thing to chew
and what you love may kill you.

The odd connection between perfection
and foolishness, like the pelican
diving for his fish.

How silly sex is.
How, having it, we glimpse
our holiness.

What I know is less and less.
What I want is more and more:

you against me—
your ferocious tenderness—

love like a star,
once small and far,
now huge, now near.

Cantaloupe

Friday I sniffed it
in the grocery store, turned it
in my hands, looking
for bruises
in the rough, webbed rind.
My mother's voice—the one
I carry always in my head—
pronounced it fine. Ripe,
but not too soft.

I bagged and bought it,
would have given it to you
for breakfast—this fruit
first grown in Cantalupo, not far
from Rome. I imagined you,
my sleepy emperor, coming
to the table in your towel toga,
digging into the luscious
orange flesh
with a golden spoon,

and afterwards,
reclining, your smile
satisfied,
imperial.

Now I open the trunk of my car
to find the cantaloupe
still there, flattened, sour,
having baked all weekend
in August's oven.

Grieving is useless,
my mother would say,
Just get another.

But why am I so certain
that no other fruit
will ever be as sweet
as that—

the one
I would have cut in half,
scooped the seeds from,
that one I would have given you
on Saturday morning?

Mammogram

Up the elevator into the slick white room
I take my sleepy twins, loose them
from their latex lair. I wonder, as I don
the paper dress—white, too, and disposable—
What do they do with the ones they cut away?
Mine are nothing remarkable, hardly
a handful if the hand is small,
but I love them and they love me back.

The technician tags each nipple with a sticker.
"Hold still," she says, as if I could move, held
in the steely grip of the big machine. I stand
on tiptoe, my heart yanked from my chest
but still shouting its worries in my ears.
"Now hold your breath," she says. "That's good.
That lump you had when you were forty,
it was benign, wasn't it?"

I think of how they grew under my nightgown,
two flowers, two girlfriends sharing their secrets;
and of the boy with his trembling fingers
reaching under my sweater, coaxing them
out of their shyness into the light of day.
How, after each baby, they swelled
and spilled their milky gifts.

Does the child, eyes closed and sucking
for all his life, have any inkling
of what will be taken away? And do you,
when you take me in your mouth,
taste that peculiar sweetness

spiced with fear, your tongue an animal
digging in the darkness for its meal, your lips
closing around what we can't know yet?

I hold my breath.

For Molly, Waiting for Breasts

They'll come in their own
sweet time, seeds sown
in the dark of sex
swelling to burst
their pods,

a curious
weight in your chest
when you lean
or turn, like pebbles
you pocketed

and then forgot.
Later,
if you're lucky, love
will stroke them tenderly
but never suck them dry

and later still
you may survive
their taking, one by one;
at best, be witness to time's
stretch and sag.

Then feel
your flattened chest,
the wizened skin,
the rising ribs,
and praise what beats beneath.

Rosebud Ruthie

Rosebud Ruthie
rides into Albuquerque
every other Saturday
in her yellow Cadillac.

He gets balder,
nobody's hero,
but still she plants a tickle
in his sandy crotch.

Rosebud Ruthie,
perpetual as wind
and sexier at sixty
than she has ever been.

"Do You Know That 20% of Women over 40 Suffer from Problems with Bladder Control?"

—from a television commercial for panty liners

Yes, and there are more of us
than you can ever know,
more of us who pee
when the key
falters in the front door lock,
our arms heavy with bags of things
that swell our bladders—
coffee and wine, for example,
but why not? We're over 40,

no longer wet behind the ears
and already out of control. We pee
before we leave for the movie,
have to go again before the previews end,
then we drink our giant Cokes
and grope across a row of knees
to find the restroom
just when the plot takes its crucial turn,
a twist we'll have to ask you about
when the movie's over but not before
another visit to the Ladies' room.

We pee when we laugh
and when we cry. We pee in the car
if city traffic stalls. On longer hauls
we cross our legs, sit
on our feet and meditate

and when that fails
we drop our pants
beside the interstate
no matter who's looking,
give the finger to the trucker, our pee
pouring onto the pavement
or into the grass, quarts of it,
gallons of it.

At night we dream we sit
on a heavenly toilet, relaxed,
unwinding, taking our time. We wake
too late to make it to the real one.
It's a proven fact, as you suspect,
that more than 20% of us
are at least 99.9% water.
There's room in us for extra
where we stored your babies,
in the hollows left by hysterectomies.

There are millions of us,
all out of control.
We'll wet your floors, your cars,
your beds, our pee
spilling from the hills,
the hinterlands, streaming
down from the dry plains,

the banks of our Mississippi
overflowing, the levees breaking
and you, passing your sandbags
man to man
as if you could stop it.

Georgia O'Keeffe in Texas

When light comes to the plains
and the evening star rises I am alone,
loving the sky.
I find a door
in the square, I paint
my way into the world—
the bulging orb,
the undulating line, the flower
opening.

I want everything all at once,
to go where the windmills
jut from the plains, to ride
into Amarillo, hear
the loud saloons, the boots
on wooden sidewalks,

then slide into Palo Duro,
the quiet canyon, as into sleep—
a slit in the nothingness,
a waterfall. I want to walk
into that wide sunset space
with the stars.

In the end,
isn't it all memory,
the flower opening, the train
trailing smoke in the Texas night?

Black Swallowtail

She hovered
over the thistle's
furry globe, her wings
trembling from the engine
of her appetite, her costume
of black velveteen and sequined
blue almost too elegant
for work. I thought,

I would like to be like that,
this butterfly for whom delight
and duty are no different.
Being
would be my only business.
Neither pride nor despair
would weigh me down.

I wouldn't dread
the shadow darkening
the grass, the stranger
stalking me,
and when the time came
I'd turn into the wind
and let it do
the work it wants to do.

Pulling Thistle

This morning
we pulled thistle from a patch of dirt
the plumber dug to reach a leaking pipe.
In just a month the prickly weed
has claimed the fresh-turned ground,
threatening our path to the pond.

It's hard not to admire
the ambition of thistle,
its determination manifest
acre over acre, hill to hollow.
Our plans are smaller—just
to clear this spot and hope for grass,
but once we're down on our knees
the whole world turns to thistle,
the job expanding each time
we pull another plant
and throw it on the pile.
We work until our gloves go stiff
with soil, until our bones
beg us to stop, both of us past
fifty and in no shape
for work like this.

Later we curl around each other,
our gnarled limbs burrowing
for something as deep as the earth
we've been digging in. I find you,
you find me, our tough stalks rise—
blindly ambitious,
sweetly defiant.

Invitation to Emily

You never left your father's house
except when every door was shut,
and then you went by open heart
into your private paradise.

How, then, can I expect you now—
a century and more away—
to come for tea in Texas, stay
for poetry, who would allow

so few for soul's society?
I offer this wide sky but know
your wisdom's wider. Should I show
you fenced-in fields, when reverie

can make a prairie all your own?
I have no velvet-headed bird
as quick, as bright, as one who stirred
your eye with his, to see the poem

from mind to page. And still I write
Dear Emily—address the envelope
to Eden, and for postage, hope
determination will suffice.

The Morning News

Too slow for the dog
who jumps ahead for butterflies
or the squirrel already
halfway up the oak,
I am going for the news
that is almost always old.
Why do I want it? Habit, mostly,
and the solace of knowing
that everything goes on without me.

Once I thought we might save it,
that world. I marched and shouted
and raised my hand-made banners.
I drew a line in the sand, dared my father
to step over, but he rubbed it out
with his practical feet. Now I am slower
to condemn his compromises.
More like him every year in face and gait,
I forgive him his mediocre sins;
I, too, bend to the dailiness of living.

In his last year, brittle, diabetic,
one leg gone and the other almost
thin as his walking stick, he hopped
to the mailbox for his morning paper.
What did it matter to him
whose heart was sputtering to a stop?
Perhaps he wanted to smell the ink,
remember his first job at *The Daily News*
when he was brash and full of faith
and truth was as clear as a headline.

I have the paper under my arm now.
Turning back, I call to the dog who leaps
from the creek with his muddy offering:
a small, half-eaten thing.
The road this morning is fringed
with orange, gold and lavender,
each flower from age-old stock
but a pure original. In the field
the thistle swells with seed, waiting
to spread its news to the world.

A Note to the Litterer

Did you come in a pick-up, alone
or drunk with your girl to neck
in this spot by the creek?
I see the tire marks

where you left the road,
stopped to pitch your bottle
over the fence. I find
your empty Buds,

the cans you crushed with those
same hands that stroked her thighs.
Your not-quite-empty Lone Stars
wink in the morning sun.

Walking home, my bag full, I hear
your litter mutter its lame excuses:
the weight of your insult
bangs against my shin.

My loathing rises like a foam
but soon goes flat
they way your tires will
if you park here again.

Winter Field, South Texas

All summer it waited for rain,
and now it waits for nothing,
black stumps of corn, what's left
of the crop after the drought.
What good can come
from this December sky,
heavy as a gun?

But then the clouds turn loose
the geese, thousands of them, until
the field swirls
in their churning blizzard.
What do they find here
that is alive, that counts
for sustenance?

Later they rise,
each bird an exclamation,
until the whole flock
moves as one unruly urge
towards heaven, ragged
and raucous as need always is.
The field's no emptier now
than before, but feels
the stillness in every clod,
the loss in every furrow.

A Dream of Horses

In the dark they left the barn
together, the old gelding
following the younger
to the far pasture.
The moon was full,
the field like snow.
They stood for a long time
looking into the sky,
lifting their heads
as if listening to the stars.
A shiver
ran the length of the young one's
nose, along his ivory blaze,
then rippled down his back,
and because
they were so close, traveled
to the other.

Deep in the cedar
the waxwings felt it,
awoke to see the flash of light,
the waves of muscles rolling
like a silvered sea, a pounding
of hooves in air, then the silent
pas de deux of flesh and fur,
bone and sinew, reach and curve,
one leading the other
(now the younger, now the older)
until the sky
could hold them no longer
and they were gone.

This Morning

We wake in a room
busy with ghosts, their voices
in breath and heartbeat, in the wind
against the window.
What they talk about is us:
our wastefulness, our wars
of selves and cities,
foul air, the ruined world.
Ex-spouses, former allies
curse our follies.
We lie together listening;
at first light rise to dress.
There'll be no peace
in the house this morning
so we walk to the pond, your arm
around my shoulder, my thumb hooked
on the back pocket of your jeans.
We pause below the berm.
Careful, quiet, we crawl to the top
and kneel together
watching the scrim of mist
lift to show us what we came for.
Weeks of rain have filled the pond again
and wild ducks cover the water—
shovelers, widgeons, a pair
of scaups and maybe something new.
Look, you whisper, passing the binoculars.
A flash of green, then yellow, blue.
I don't have time to focus before
they turn and fly, a hundred wings

whirring overhead until they disappear
behind the neighbor's hill.
Darling, if this won't save us,
nothing will.